Especially for

For my Dear Sister - Ilene

From

Betty

Date

6 - 5 - 13

© 2011 by Wanda E. Brunstetter.

ISBN 978-1-61626-197-9

All scripture quotations are taken from the King James Version of the Bible.

Cover image © Doyle Yoder, www.dypinc.com
Art on pages 91, 92, 96, 99, 100, 103, 104 © Doyle Yoder
Art on pages 4, 27, 48, 71, 95, 119, 140 © Richard Brunstetter

Published by Barbour Publishing, Inc., P.O. Box 719, Uhrichsville, Ohio 44683, www.barbourbooks.com

Our mission is to publish and distribute inspirational products offering exceptional value and biblical encouragement to the masses.

ecpa Member of the
Evangelical Christian
Publishers Association

Printed in China.

Inspiring Thoughts
from the Simple Life

WANDA E. BRUNSTETTER

BARBOUR
PUBLISHING

*May you discover a sense of peace and joy in the practical,
yet inspiring wisdom found in this little book—along with a desire
to live life a little more simply. . .and a little closer to God.*

God is pleased when we show hospitality.
After all, for some people, our friendship and
hospitality may be the only Jesus they will ever see.

*Be not forgetful to entertain strangers: for thereby
some have entertained angels unawares.*
HEBREWS 13:2

May others know we belong to
Jesus by the love they see in us.

⸎

Lamps do not talk; they shine.

May we always remember to call on God
whenever we have a need.

If you are too busy to pray,
you are busier than God wants you to be.

Not only are we blessed when someone helps bear our burdens, but the one who helps is blessed, too.

Timely good deeds are nicer than afterthoughts.

Many times the best lesson is learned from encouragement.
Is there someone you might encourage today?

He that is slow to wrath is of great understanding:
but he that is hasty of spirit exalteth folly.

PROVERBS 14:29

God never forces us to do anything against our will.
His love is unconditional. He wants everyone
to come willingly to Him, and He will never
force us or hold us captive.

The human heart, at whatever age,
opens only to the heart that opens in return.

A simple thing such as a rainbow in the sky can remind us
that God is there constantly, loving and protecting us.
He will always keep His promises.

There's a rainbow of hope that is shining above,
reminding us of God's endless love.

God has promised to forgive our sins.
All we have to do is ask.

It should be our main interest in this
world to secure an interest in the next.

There is strength in unity, for people working together
can do many things that people alone can't do.

Many hands make work seem lighter,
especially if they are proficiently skilled hands.

Great joy comes in giving to others
from the bounty God has given.

While seeking happiness for others,
we unconsciously find it for ourselves.

Whenever we are confused or make mistakes, we have
the assurance that God is always there and we can call on Him,
day or night, even for the simplest tasks.

Let prayer be the key to the day and the bolt to the night.

God will give us the strength and energy
to make it through the hardest of times.

When we have nothing left but God,
we will find that He is enough.

If we love one another, God dwelleth in us,
and his love is perfected in us.

I JOHN 4:12

Life without love is like a day without light.

We should thank God daily
for His love and protection.

God does not shield us *from* life's storms;
He shelters us *in* life's storms.

If we become concerned with things that *might* happen,
we will lose sight of the joy God has given us today. . . .
Our future is in God's hands, and He will see us through.

*You can't see around the corners,
but God can.*

When you allow God to control your life and put your trust in Him, He will give you internal and eternal peace.

❧❧❧

Faith is not belief without proof,
but trust without reservation.

The next time you hear a bird sing, why not use it as a reminder to lift your voice in praise to God?

When you sing your own praises, you always get the tune too high; when you sing God's praises, you can never go high enough.

If we trust in our own wisdom, we might make a mistake; but if we turn to God for guidance, He will help us make a wise decision.

If you can't have the best of everything, make the best of everything you have.

Even when the burdens of life take us down,
through Christ we can be renewed in spirit every day.

*God does not spare us trials,
but He helps us overcome them.*

The next time you feel stressed,
a good antidote is to take time out to reflect
on everything God has given to you.

And my people shall be satisfied
with my goodness, saith the LORD.
JEREMIAH 31:14

We are God's children, and when we are in danger,
He hides us in the cleft of the rock, under His wing,
and in the shadow of His hand.

When the world around you is crumbling,
God is the rock on which you can stand.

Jesus wants us to seek His will and follow Him so that He can meet our physical and spiritual needs.

If we let God guide,
He will provide.

Every child is precious in
God's sight—including you!

Every child of God has
a special place in His plan.

Children see the world differently than most adults.
They not only notice things but also will often take
the time to study, touch, smell, and even taste the many
astonishing things God has created for our enjoyment.

Don't overlook life's small joys
while searching for the big ones.

Only God can give the kind of joy
that changes lives and reflects His love.

Happy hearts make happy homes.

Prayer and faith bring the peace of God.

When worry knocks at the door, send faith to answer it—
and you'll find no one there.

Keep your priorities straight on the things
that matter most—on things that count for eternity.

Success comes to the person who does today
what she's thinking of doing tomorrow.

For the L<small>ORD</small> seeth not as man seeth; for man looketh on the outward appearance, but the L<small>ORD</small> looketh on the heart.

1 S<small>AMUEL</small> 16:7

Others may be deaf to our words,
but they are never blind to our actions.

The trials we encounter
reveal our true character.

No matter how many trials come our way,
God is only a prayer away.

When family members pray together
and work together, a lot can be accomplished
and relationships become stronger.

No person can do everything,
but each one can do something.

It's always best to deal with
problems in a loving way.

❧

You can't speak a kind word too soon.

The best remedy for remorse: Seek God's forgiveness,
apologize to whomever we have wronged,
then forgive ourselves and move on.

Forgive someone—maybe even yourself.
It will set you free.

Rather than complaining or feeling sorry for ourselves,
we can learn to rely on God and be content
with whatever He provides.

Find contentment in enjoying the present season
instead of dreaming about the next.

Always strive to speak kind words
to everyone you meet.

Nothing is opened more times
by mistake than the mouth.

There is no scale or chart on earth
to measure what a true friend is worth.

A man that hath friends must shew himself friendly:
and there is a friend that sticketh closer than a brother.
PROVERBS 18:24

There are times when we don't know specifically how to help someone in need. Even when we can't help in a physical sense, we can still pray. Is there someone you should be praying for today?

The best form of exercise is to touch the floor regularly with your knees.

God blesses through His provisions—
the giver and the receiver alike.

People seldom get dizzy doing good turns.

God wants us to reap the harvest by telling others
about His Son through our words and deeds.

Have your harvest tools ready,
and God will find work for you.

If we must boast, then let's boast in God,
who has redeemed us and strengthens us each day.

*The man who has a right
to boast does not have to.*

If we took the time to become better acquainted with
our neighbors and were willing to help in times of need,
how much better our world would become.

When you help someone up a hill,
you're that much nearer the top yourself.

Worshipping with our friends and family not only draws us closer to them, but also to God.

Christians are like chunks of coal:
Together they glow; apart they die out.

Taking the time to relax and enjoy the beauty of God's
creation can restore and renew our tired bodies,
as well as our minds.

It is not the load that breaks us down.
It's the way we carry it.

I will instruct thee and teach thee in the way which thou shalt go:
I will guide thee with mine eye.

PSALM 32:8

God is always there to guide, direct,
and help us through our mistakes.

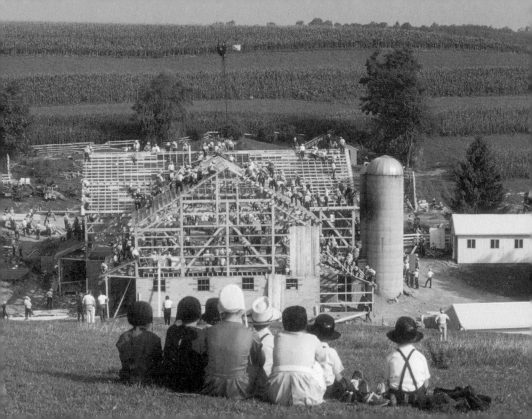

By reading the Bible and following God's instruction manual,
our lives are reshaped so we can become better than we were before.

People get into trouble when they think
they can handle life without God.

During difficult times our help should come from the Lord,
for He has the remedy to all our problems.

Never say never, and never give up.

Despite discouragements and difficult problems,
it's important for us to forge ahead
and keep walking with Jesus.

❧ ∽∽∽ ❧

*Trust God to move your mountain,
but keep on digging.*

If we read the Bible and follow God's guidelines,
everything will work out in the end.

It's impossible to drive in the wrong direction
and arrive at the right destination.

God knows for certain
what we can only imagine.

The things I can see help me trust
God for the things I cannot see.

Life's most strengthening experience is the awareness of God's presence in our lives, no matter what difficulties come our way.

Keep looking up, for God is looking down.

*Let's remember to thank God
every day for His faithfulness.*

The angel of the LORD encampeth round about
them that fear him, and delivereth them.

PSALM 34:7

God will guide, direct, and help us find our way back to Him.
All we need to do is call on His name.

Life without Christ is a hopeless end.
With Christ it's an endless hope.

If we keep our eyes on our heavenly Father,
distressing, discouraging thoughts will lessen.

Remedy for discouragement: Reach up as far as you can,
and God will reach down the rest of the way.

God doesn't want us to lose faith or give way to despair.
He wants us to press on with patience,
always hoping for the best, always trusting Him.

Patience is a word that carries a lot of wait.

Someday, when we meet God face-to-face,
we will receive our reward for faithfulness.

Blessed are those who give without remembering
and receive without forgetting.

It's all right to remember and treasure things from the past,
but God wants us to enjoy each new day and to live it
to the fullest, with gratitude.

It is better to look forward and prepare
than to look back and despair.

Keeping our focus on God will help us make
wise choices and keep us from being led astray.

A man seldom knows what he can do
until he tries to undo what he did.

We like the feeling of independence, but there are times when we
need others to help with things we're unable to do,
or to help us overcome temptations.

*He who stands on his own
strength will never stand.*

Two are better than one; because they have a good reward for their labour. For if they fall, the one will lift up his fellow: but woe to him that is alone when he falleth; for he hath not another to help him up.

ECCLESIASTES 4:9–10

A tree needs more than one branch to be productive, and so do we. Jesus (the vine) should be our primary help, and the branches (others) are there to help us stay on the right track.

Looking on the brighter side of things—
thinking constructive, pleasant, positive thoughts—
can change lives by drawing positive results our way.

*Every sunrise is a new message from God,
and every sunset His signature.*

When we give verbal expression for our appreciation,
it makes us feel nearly as good as it does the one
who receives the appreciation.

If you can't be thankful for what you receive,
be thankful for what you escape.

How long has it been since you told
someone you appreciate them?

When was the last time you told God
how much you appreciate Him?

Real beauty comes from within.

What makes us beautiful to God is when
He sees us smiling, treating others kindly,
and showing His love through our actions.

What did you see when you
looked in the mirror today?

Of all the things you wear,
your expression is the most important.

*Others can't see Jesus until
we let our light shine for Him.*

God gave us the sun, moon, and stars that we may see
the beauty of His creation; and He, being light Himself,
guides and directs those who follow Him, as we direct
others to Jesus, the sweetest light of all.

As a bright sunbeam comes into every window,
so comes a love born of God's care for every need.

This then is the message which we have heard of him,
and declare unto you, that God is light,
and in Him is no darkness at all.

1 JOHN 1:5

Avoid trying to "sell" someone on Jesus.

By allowing people to see God's light and love in you, they will be more apt to come to Him. Let the work He's doing in your life do the "talking."

Even though God knows our needs before we ask,
He wants us to seek His help.

God may answer quickly or make us wait, but we can
be sure that He will answer, according to His will.

God loves us so much that He sent His Son to die for our sins.
Shouldn't we find ways to show our love to others?

We can show others we love them in many ways—
through a sacrificial gift, a kind word, or a friendly smile.

Even during the most distressing times, the Good Shepherd watches over His people and is always with us.

It's comforting to know that our heavenly Father always knows where His children are, even when we don't know we are lost.

Accept what you must and change what you can.
Look to the future with a sense of hope
and thank God for each new day, for we really do
have so much to be grateful for.

*The seed of discouragement will
not grow in a thankful heart.*

Knowing that God can use all things for His good is more
than reason enough for us to give thanks in everything.

Do you want to please God and get to know Him better?
Then remember to tell Him thank You every time you pray.

Life can be difficult at times, but nothing can separate us from God's love. God gives every believer a sense of peace if they keep their eyes on Him and not on the things of this world.

It's comforting to know that God keeps the earth rotating and the seasons changing. He makes the sun rise every morning and sets the sun at just the right time each evening. All that God does should remind us that He is in control, which will give us a perfect peace.

*For whosoever shall give you a cup of water
to drink in my name, because ye belong to Christ,
verily I say unto you, he shall not lose his reward.*

MARK 9:41

Hospitality seems easier when we are with family and friends,
but God reminds us to entertain those outside our familiar circle.

There are many times when we are unable to do anything about our external circumstances. Those are the times that we need to remember to call on God, for He is only a prayer away.

God feels our pain and sorrow and is always there to offer comfort when we endure sorrows.

Children are one of God's special gifts,
and so is each new day He gives us.

Taking time to think about the blessings God has given us
can help redirect our thoughts and help us prioritize.

Just as a baby is precious to his parents and siblings,
so are we precious to our heavenly Father.

*God will be a father to us,
and to our sons and daughters.*

God made each one of us unique.

While we may look similar to someone else, the way we act is proof of who we really are—and whose we are.

To make friends and keep them, we must learn
to be a friend by showing ourselves friendly
and being there when our friends have a need.

Wouldn't it be nice to know that when people think
about us, they will remember the good things we've
done for them? Likewise, it's good for us to appreciate
the friends who have meant so much to us.

It should never come as a surprise when God provides.

~~~~~

God sometimes uses other people to bless us with things we need, and when we thank them, we should also remember to thank God for His unexpected gifts.

God is all-knowing, all-loving, all-powerful, all-forgiving,
and He will show you His plan for your life if you trust Him.

The LORD is good, a strong hold in the day of trouble;
and he knoweth them that trust in him.

NAHUM 1:7

*The opportunity to worship
with others is a blessing.*

While it's true that we can feel close to God in many different
settings, the gathering together with other believers gives
us a common bond and dispels loneliness.

Even if you can't leave the house for a time of renewal, remember to pause several times during your busy day.

Take a few deep breaths, close your eyes, and visualize yourself sitting in a quiet place beside the Lord.

Each day of our lives we take steps through the choices we make.
Some are baby steps; others are giant steps.

The steps we take today
determine our tomorrows.

With God, nothing is impossible.

The Bible is an instruction manual that must be carefully, thoughtfully, and prayerfully read in order to understand the direction God wants us to take in our daily walk with Him.

God has given us many wonderful things to praise Him for—
answered prayer, our daily provisions, good health, family,
friends, and most of all, His Son, Jesus.

Teach me thy way, O LORD, and lead me in a plain path.
PSALM 27:11